Would You Rather Game Book for Kids

500 Challenging, Funny, Silly, Weird, Gross and Random Questions Fun for Family, Teens and Children

SILLY SALAMANDER

WOULD YOU RATHER GAME BOOK FOR KIDS

© **Copyright 2019 – Silly Salamander All rights reserved.**

The content contained within this book may not be reproduced, duplicated or transmitted without direct written permission from the author or the publisher.

Under no circumstances will any blame or legal responsibility be held against the publisher, or author, for any damages, reparation, or monetary loss due to the information contained within this book. Either directly or indirectly.

Legal Notice:

This book is copyright protected. This book is only for personal use. You cannot amend, distribute, sell, use, quote or paraphrase any part, or the content within this book, without the consent of the author or publisher.

Disclaimer Notice:

Please note the information contained within this document is for educational and entertainment purposes only. All effort has been executed to present accurate, up to date, and reliable, complete information. No warranties of any kind are declared or implied. Readers acknowledge that the author is not engaging in the rendering of legal, financial, medical or professional advice. The content within this book has been derived from various sources. Please consult a licensed professional before attempting any techniques outlined in this book.

By reading this document, the reader agrees that under no circumstances is the author responsible for any losses, direct or indirect, which are incurred as a result of the use of the information contained within this document, including, but not limited to, — errors, omissions, or inaccuracies.

WOULD YOU RATHER GAME BOOK FOR KIDS

TABLE OF CONTENTS

1 **Introduction** — Pg #8

2 **Instructions** — Pg #10

3 **Silly & Funny Questions!** — Pg #12

4 **Difficult Questions!** — Pg #25

5 **Gross Questions!** — Pg #32

6 **Food Questions!** — Pg #38

7 **Random Questions!** — Pg #45

8 **Conclusion** — Pg #59

WOULD YOU RATHER GAME BOOK FOR KIDS

INTRODUCTION

Looking for an exciting book that can give you hours of fun? You've come to the right place! We've spent long days and nights putting the most interesting and entertaining "Would You Rather?" questions together and we hope you enjoy using this book as much as we enjoyed writing it.

We'd like to thank you for buying our book and we are so excited for you to start using it. We love playing "Would You Rather" during family get-togethers, class trips, and sleepovers with friends. You can use this game with your very best friends or as an icebreaker with people you've just met. This is especially fun to do in a party to get to know the other guests better. Even long car trips become enjoyable when you play this game with your family.

Our questions will make you laugh, and some will make you think hard. We hope you discover something new about yourself and about the people you play this game with. The next section will give you some guidelines and tell you how to play. Have fun!

INSTRUCTIONS

This game can be played any way you like. It can be as simple as a casual Q&A in a group, with each person taking a turn to answer the questions. If you have a big group and need more structure, here are some guidelines you can follow:

1) **Split yourselves into two teams**

Pick a team that will start. The other team will read the first question for the starting team to answer. The two teams will take turns answering for every question in the book.

2) **The answering team must choose one of the options for each question**

The team must decide on one answer per question and explain why they chose that answer.

3) Keep going until one of the teams can't choose an answer

If a team can't decide on an answer, that team loses.

The great thing is, the main objective of this game is to have fun so it's always win-win for everyone, no matter who "loses." With so many questions to answer, this game can be as short or as long you need it to be. The possibilities are endless! What are you waiting for? Start the book and get ready to have a blast!

SILLY AND FUNNY QUESTIONS

1. Would you rather you rather have pink hair or purple hair?
2. Would you rather pet a poisonous snake or swim with an electric eel?
3. Would you rather have a belly button on your forehead or a bellybutton on your chin?
4. Would you rather only be able to wear a swimsuit for the rest of your life or formal wear for the rest of your life?
5. Would you rather be a flying unicorn or a dragon?
6. Would you rather wear a superhero cape or wear an eye patch?
7. Would you rather have three ears or only one ear?
8. Would you rather have a pig nose or whiskers on your face?

9. Would you rather wear clown makeup every day for a year or dress like a clown every day for a year?
10. Would you rather cuddle a giant teddy bear or cuddle your mom?
11. Would you rather be a table or a chair?
12. Would you rather be really tall or really strong?
13. Would you rather sneeze cheese or laugh jellybeans?
14. Would you rather watch your favorite movie every day or play your favorite video game every day?
15. Would you rather paint an entire house using one cotton swab or paint an entire skyscraper using one paintbrush?
16. Would you rather have to sing every time you talk or dance every time you move?
17. Would you rather have an ear where your nose is or noses where your ears are?
18. Would you rather have only one leg or one hand?
19. Would you rather wake up with a giraffe neck or an elephant trunk?
20. Would you rather wear a tiger print shirt every day or a giraffe print shirt every day?

21. Would you rather only wear green clothes for the rest of your life or only red clothes for the rest of your life?
22. Would you rather eat all your food using only a spoon or using only a fork?
23. Would you rather have to always wear a thick scarf or always have to wear thick gloves?
24. Would you rather eat a hamburger for breakfast or cereal for dessert?
25. Would you rather sleep on a thin mat on a floor or ten mattresses?
26. Would you rather have to cartwheel or walk on your hands to get anywhere?
27. Would you rather have hair that is always straight or always super curly?
28. Would you rather have long eyelashes that reach your cheeks or long eyebrows that below your eyes?
29. Would you rather be able to only communicate using drawings or by morse code?
30. Would you rather give a 30-minute speech in front of your entire school or work in your school cafeteria for one week?

31. Would you rather drive a beautiful, sleek sports car that was unreliable or an ugly, dented, old car that never broke down?
32. Would you rather see a hamster as big as an elephant or see an elephant as big as a hamster?
33. Would you rather have a really big tummy or a really big butt?
34. Would you rather sleep with no pillow under your head or have to sleep with five pillows under your head?
35. Would you rather be the star dancer of a show or watch a dance performance?
36. Would you rather lose all your hair or lose all your teeth?
37. Would you rather have a very long neck or no neck at all?
38. Would you rather wear shoes with laces that keep on getting untied or wear socks that are always falling down?
39. Would you rather have a pet tiger or a pet orangutan?
40. Would you rather all your clothes be oversized or be really tight?

41. Would you rather be always missing one sock or missing one shoe?
42. Would you rather be a cheerleader or play sports?
43. Would you rather see a giant snail or a giant grasshopper?
44. Would you rather have four eyebrows or no eyebrows?
45. Would you rather go to school for two months a year for five years or ten months straight in one year?
46. Would you rather be a pet dog or be a pet cat?
47. Would you rather be a magician or a circus performer?
48. Would you rather have a head the size of a grapefruit or a head the size of a watermelon?
49. Would you rather moo like a cow before speaking or bark like a dog before speaking?
50. Would you rather wear neon pink shoes all the time or neon yellow shoes all the time?
51. Would you rather find ten snakes or one tiger in your room?
52. Would you rather have a brand-new giant TV that you can use once a week or a small old TV that you can use every day?

53. Would you rather have butterfly wings or a horse tail?
54. Would you rather own a robot or your own spaceship?
55. Would you rather have fingers for legs or legs for fingers?
56. Would you rather wake up in the morning looking like a giraffe or a kangaroo?
57. Would you rather walk around with messy hair or walk around mismatched clothes?
58. Would you rather go on a hike barefoot or go to the beach with a coat?
59. Would you rather be a hamster or a guinea pig?
60. Would you rather be part of the Avengers or Justice League?
61. Would you rather be able to travel in time or be able to go on a space adventure?
62. Would you rather have flowers growing on your hair or have flowers growing out of your bellybutton?
63. Would you rather fly riding a broomstick or fly on the back of a dragon?
64. Would you rather turn into a bear once a week or turn into a bird once a week?

65. Would you rather have a finger coming out of your one nostril or a finger coming out of one ear?
66. Would you rather cry when you hear something funny or laugh when you hear something sad?
67. Would you rather have fast-growing hair that needs a haircut every week or slow-growing hair that needs one haircut a year?
68. Would you rather live in a bright green house or live in a bright pink house?
69. Would you rather wake up with a tail or wake up with horns?
70. Would you rather always have to wear flip-flops all the time or have to wear winter boots all the time?
71. Would you rather live beside a jungle full of wild animals or beside a river full of crocodiles?
72. Would you rather wake up with your dad's face or your mom's face?
73. Would you rather eat cold food all the time or eat hot food all the time?
74. Would you rather drink from a bowl all the time or a baby bottle all the time?
75. Would you rather your laugh sounds like a monkey or your laugh sounds like a rooster?

76. Would you rather eat with chopsticks all the time or eat with your hands all the time?
77. Would you rather have pink skin or pink eyes?
78. Would you rather be a spider or be a mosquito?
79. Would you rather live in the basement of a house or the attic of a house?
80. Would you rather have to blink sixty times a minute or not blink for one minute?
81. Would you rather have a pet iguana or a pet turtle?
82. Would you rather have to wear a red vest all the time or red suspenders all the time?
83. Would you rather always say something funny when someone asks you a serious question or say something serious when someone asks you a funny question?
84. Would you rather walk around wearing a witch's hat or holding a witch's broom?
85. Would you rather wear a Halloween costume every day or dress like the Easter bunny every day?
86. Would you rather be garden snail or a sea slug?
87. Would you rather have giant ears or have a giant nose?
88. Would you rather have wear a baseball hat all the time or have to wear sunglasses all the time?

89. Would you rather be a lion tamer or a bear trainer?
90. Would you rather work in a circus or work in an aquarium?
91. Would you rather write ten thank notes a day or never get another present?
92. Would you rather always wait in long lines to enter a store or have to go to a store in the middle of the night to shop?
93. Would you rather have extra long teeth or extra long fingers?
94. Would you rather be a sea turtle or a land tortoise?

95. Would you rather go to the playground eight time in one month or go to an amusement park once in one month?
96. Would you rather swim in a huge swimming pool or swim in a small lake?
97. Would you rather live in a house with swimming pool or own your own motorcycle?
98. Would you rather have a big yard with only grass or have a small yard with a swing set?
99. Would you rather own one great toy that you'll like to play with for five years or five toys that you'll only like to play with for one year?

100. Would you rather have a cabin in the woods or a small house on the beach?
101. Would you rather see a Komodo dragon when walking to school or see a mountain lion when walking to school?
102. Would you rather have a car that can turn into a submarine or a car that can turn into a helicopter?
103. Would you rather go to the mall with your parents or go to the park with your friends?

104. Would you rather have to wear a wet t-shirt or have to wear a wet pair of pants?
105. Would you rather grow a unicorn horn or grow dragon wings?
106. Would you rather have a pet dog you can talk to or a pet dog that can do your chores?
107. Would you rather sleep outside when it's raining or sleep outside when it's snowing?
108. Would you rather live in a treehouse or live in a fort made of branches?
109. Would you rather have a self-refilling glass that never runs out of soda or a self-refilling bowl that never runs out of popcorn?

110. Would you rather spend the day with your baby sibling or spend the day with your grandmother?

111. Would you rather have a cat that barks like a dog or a dog that meows like a cat?

112. Would you rather have a pet parrot or a pet monkey?

113. Would you rather be a squirrel or a raccoon?

114. Would you rather go home from school every day to eat lunch or go home one hour early every day?

115. Would you rather live in a house full of plants or in a house full of pets?

116. Would you rather share a room with your parents or share a room with your siblings?

117. Would you rather be stepped on by a horse or be thrown by a gorilla?

118. Would you rather have a tiny baby head or tiny baby legs?

119. Would you rather not have school every Friday or not have school every Monday?

120. Would you rather own your own roller coaster at home or your own kid-size train at home?

121. Would you rather have elephant ears or elephant tusks?
122. Would you rather be able to become really, really tiny or become really, really big?
123. Would you rather be made of metal or made of plastic?

124. Would you rather grow octopus legs or caterpillar legs?
125. Would you rather shoot fire from your hands or shoot ice from your eyes?
126. Would you rather kiss a frog or kiss a snake?
127. Would you rather have time machine or a magic wand?
128. Would you rather have all the books that you want or all the toys that you want?
129. Would you rather be shot out of a cannon or jump out of the plane?
130. Would you rather be a character in your favorite book or a character in your favorite video game?
131. Would you rather be a tall tree or a pretty flower?

132. **Would you rather be able to talk to animals or be able to fly?**

DIFFICULT QUESTIONS

1. Would you rather have a remote control that fast forwarded your life or a remote control that rewound it?
2. Would you rather be invisible or be able to fly?
3. Would you rather live in a home with no electricity or a home with no running water?
4. Would you rather be completely alone for one year or never alone for one year?
5. Would you rather be blind for the rest of your life or mute for the rest of your life?
6. Would you rather win one million dollars today or ten million dollars in ten years?
7. Would you rather live without music or live without video games?
8. Would you rather have the ability to see through walls or have the ability to walk through walls?

9. Would you rather go on a luxurious two-week vacation with cousins you don't get along with or a cheaper two-day vacation with friends?
10. Would you rather move countries every year for the next ten years or live in the same apartment for the next ten years?
11. Would you rather lose your sense of touch or your sense of smell?
12. Would you rather have three free wishes or be the richest person on Earth?
13. Would you rather have lunch with your parents for one hour every day or only see them on a three week vacation each year?
14. Would you rather help yourself first or help others first?
15. Would you rather live alone on a desert island or live in a busy city in a house with ten strangers?
16. Would you rather have no TV or no Internet?
17. Would you rather take a trip around the world but never be able to stop to see anything or be unable to ever leave the city you live in again?
18. Would you rather be always ten minutes late or always one hour early?

19. Would you rather forget how to read or forget how to write?
20. Would you rather anything you touch turn to gold or turn to diamonds?
21. Would you rather be able to understand what animals are thinking or read people's minds?
22. Would you rather stay home for one month straight or only go home for two hours a day for one month?
23. Would you rather be an only child or the middle of child of seven children?
24. Would you rather be hungry all the time or thirsty all the time?
25. Would you rather never open your eyes or never open your mouth?
26. Would you rather be stuck on a desert island alone or stuck on a desert island with your worst enemy?
27. Would you rather be incredibly funny or incredibly smart?
28. Would you rather stay a kid until you turn 80 years old or turn 40 years old tomorrow?
29. Would you rather have a piggy bank that doubles any money you put in or have $10 under your pillow every morning?

30. Would you rather have only one great friend or five good friends?
31. Would you rather go to school for five years straight or never go to school again for the rest of your life?
32. Would you rather lose your sense of taste or your sense of smell?
33. Would you rather remember everything you read or be able solve any Math problem?
34. Would you rather find the cure to a deadly illness or find the end to world hunger?
35. Would you rather babysit a baby that doesn't stop crying or stay up all night to help a family member you don't know very well?
36. Would you rather be class president or team captain of the basketball team?
37. Would you rather tell someone bad news or be the one to receive bad news?
38. Would you rather have a new adventure every day for a month or do the exact same things every day for a month?
39. Would you rather have two great life-long friends or make lots of new acquaintances every year?

40. Would you rather be very good-looking with a moderate amount of money or average-looking with lots of money?
41. Would you rather feel too hot all the time or too cold all the time?
42. Would you rather have your own small bathroom but share a big bedroom with your sibling or have your own small bedroom but share a big bathroom with your sibling?
43. Would you rather live 50 years in the past or 50 years in the future?
44. Would you rather be able to find anything that was lost or every time you touched someone they would be unable to lie?
45. Would you rather have one job that you like for the rest of your life or try a new job every year?
46. Would you rather be rich or be famous?
47. Would you rather be the inventor of the Iphone or the inventor of the light bulb?
48. Would you rather be friends with a famous actor or be friends with a famous chef?
49. Would you rather go to college out of state or go to college driving distance from your home?

50. Would you rather read one book a day for the rest of your life or never read a book again?
51. Would you rather listen to the same five songs every day for the rest of your life or never listen to songs again for the rest of your life?
52. Would you rather have to spend 12 hours a day in front of the computer or never be able to use a computer again?
53. Would you rather live in a house with electricity only from 7 am to 7 pm or live in a house with electricity only from 7 pm to 7 am?
54. Would you rather give all your savings to your parents or give all your savings to your best friend?
55. Would you rather spend time with your mom's side of the family or your dad's side of the family?
56. Would you rather work as a housekeeper for a person with a messy house or the only nanny of four young children?
57. Would you rather be a great gift giver or always like the gifts you receive?
58. Would you rather be able to control weather or control time?
59. Would you rather be a famous villain or an unknown superhero?

60. Would you rather be a great scientist or a great president?
61. Would you rather work volunteer at a daycare or volunteer in a nursing home?
62. Would you rather be the funny one in a group of friends or the smart one in a group of friends?
63. Would you rather be a principal of your school or the coach of your basketball team?

GROSS QUESTIONS

1. Would you rather brush your teeth with a dirty toothbrush or wipe your butt with dirty toilet paper?
2. Would you rather lick the bottom of your shoes or eat your boogers?
3. Would you rather sleep on a pillow that smells like fish or have to wear clothes that smell like fish?
4. Would you rather have to wake up to poop twice a night or wake up to pee four times a night?
5. Would you rather drink an entire glass of apple juice mixed with pee or drink a teaspoon of pure pee?
6. Would you rather be covered in worms or covered in ants?
7. Would you rather scratch your butt in public or scratch your armpit in public?
8. Would you rather find a cockroach in your pizza or a cockroach inside your shoe?

9. Would you rather chew a piece of gum you found on the street or a piece of gum from your friend's mouth?
10. Would you rather drink sour milk or eat rotten eggs?
11. Would you rather have a booger hanging from your nose for the rest of your life or earwax planted on your earlobes?
12. Would you rather drop your phone into the toilet or drop your favorite bracelet in the toilet?
13. Would you rather produce farts that smell good or constantly fart that have no smell at all?
14. Would you rather find spider eggs inside your bed or a trail of red ants inside your bed?
15. Would you rather your hands be dirty all the time of your feet be dirty all the time?
16. Would you rather have to eat raw chicken or eat raw beef?
17. Would you rather someone cough on you or sneeze on you?
18. Would you rather eat worms only for three days or not eat anything for three days?
19. Would you rather smell like sweat socks or smell like a skunk?

20. Would you drink a raw egg or a cup of cooking oil?
21. Would you rather eat your fingernails or eat your toenails?
22. Would you rather step on something smelly and sticky or something wet and sticky?
23. Would you rather pee in a bucket or pee in the woods?
24. Would you rather wipe your face with a towel that hasn't been washed for a month or wipe your face with a stranger's used towel?
25. Would you rather dip your face into a plate of vinegar or a plate of bbq sauce?
26. Would you rather brush your teeth with shampoo or brush your teeth with a bar of soap?
27. Would you rather wear the same set of clothes for a week straight or wear different dirty clothes every day for a week?
28. Would you rather lick the bathroom floor or lick a toilet seat?
29. Would you rather live in a house with a smelly bathroom or live in a house with a smelly bedroom?
30. Would you rather clean the bathroom with a toothbrush or clean a garbage can with a toothbrush?

31. Would you rather grow long underarm hairs or grow long hairs on your fingers?
32. Would you rather have a big pimple in between your eyes or five small pimples on your cheek?
33. Would you rather step on slime or get slime stuck in your hair?
34. Would you rather eat a moldy piece of cheese or drink curdled milk?
35. Would you rather have bad breath or underarms that smell bad?
36. Would you rather swallow a teaspoon of your own blood or a teaspoon of your own pee?
37. Would you rather have a boil on the tip of your nose or a boil in the middle of your forehead?
38. Would you rather take out the garbage with bare hands or wash the garbage can with bare hands?
39. Would you rather eat cake that was made with salt instead of sugar or meatloaf made with sugar instead of salt?
40. Would you rather have snot coming out of your nose all the time or have something always stuck in the middle of your two front teeth?
41. Would you rather eat fried insects or eat fried worms?

42. Would you rather use mayonnaise as toothpaste or use mayonnaise as shampoo?
43. Would you rather fart every time you stand up from a chair or burp every time you took a step?
44. Would you rather get peed on by a dog or step on dog poop while barefoot?
45. Would you rather have to smell your classmate's fart at the beginning of each class or have your classmate smell your fart at the beginning of each class?
46. Would you rather wear a shirt smell like a wet dog or wear a shirt that had stains on it?
47. Would you rather clean up a classmate's puke or clean up a classmate's pee?
48. Would you rather have your hands completely covered in hair completely or your neck completely covered in hair?
49. Would you rather eat cooked frog's legs or a cooked pig's ear?
50. Would you rather touch a caterpillar or have a moth land in your eye?
51. Would you rather clean someone's ears or clean someone's nose?

52. Would you rather sleep beside a stinky dog or sleep beside a cat's litter box?
53. Would you rather find a spider on your face when you wake up or a cockroach on your face when you wake up?
54. Would you rather fix a clogged toilet or fix a clogged shower drain?
55. Would you rather swallow a mosquito or swallow a fly?
56. Would you rather eat moldy bread or a rotten apple?
57. Would you rather find hair in your food or a fingernail in your food?
58. Would you rather see a rat in your kitchen or see a rat in your bedroom?
59. Would you rather be covered in mud or covered in slime?
60. Would you rather have booger-flavored ice cream or earwax-flavored ice cream?

FOOD QUESTIONS

1. Would you rather eat a dozen doughnuts or a dozen cookies in one sitting?
2. Would you rather eat only pizza or only French fries for the rest of your life?
3. Would you rather drink a glass of garlic juice or a glass of onion juice?
4. Would you rather eat a bowl of mustard or a bowl of mayonnaise?
5. Would you rather eat a chocolate bar or a lollipop?
6. Would you rather eat something really sour or really spicy?
7. Would you rather drink hot chocolate or chocolate milk?
8. Would you rather eat pancakes every day for breakfast or pizza every day for dinner?
9. Would you rather eat an entire cake or an entire tub of ice cream?

10. Would you rather eat a whole pizza or an entire bucket of fried chicken?
11. Would you rather eat a year's worth of French fries in one night or never eat French fries again?
12. Would you rather eat an orange or drink orange juice?
13. Would you rather eat a bag of chips or a bowl of popcorn?
14. Would you rather eat ten popsicles or ten ice cream cones?
15. Would you rather eat extra-spicy spaghetti or extra-sweet spaghetti?
16. Would you rather eat apple pie or blueberry cheesecake?
17. Would you rather eat a plate of steamed broccoli or a plate of steamed cauliflower?
18. Would you rather only drink apple juice for the rest of your life or only drink milk for the rest of your life?
19. Would you rather eat only junk food for one month or eat only vegetables for one month?
20. Would you rather eat a can of dog food or a can of cat food?

21. Would you rather eat a banana sandwich with mayonnaise or eat a banana sandwich with ketchup?
22. Would you rather eat only asparagus for the rest of your life or only Brussel sprouts for the rest of your life?
23. Would you rather eat a ham sandwich or a cheese sandwich?
24. Would you rather eat clams or eat shrimps?
25. Would you rather eat a bowl of spaghetti sauce without noodles or a bowl of noodles without sauce?
26. Would you rather eat fish-flavored cookies or garlic-flavored ice cream?
27. Would you rather give up eating sweets or give up eating fast food?
28. Would you rather eat a burrito or eat a taco?
29. Would you rather have nuts in your ice cream or sprinkles in your ice cream?
30. Would you rather eat mint-flavored chocolate or orange-flavored chocolate?
31. Would you rather eat blueberries or strawberries?
32. Would you rather drink iced tea or lemonade?
33. Would you rather eat cotton candy or churros?

34. Would you rather eat chocolate cake or chocolate pudding?
35. Would you rather eat mint vanilla ice cream or strawberry ice cream?
36. Would you rather be good at cooking or good at baking?
37. Would you rather have to drink twelve glasses of water a day or only one glass of water a day?
38. Would you rather eat pancakes or waffles?
39. Would you rather eat a raw turnip or a raw bell pepper?
40. Would you rather eat a salad or eat cooked vegetables?
41. Would you rather chicken soup or clam chowder?
42. Would you rather have to eat all your food with too much salt or all your food with too much pepper?
43. Would you rather eat bacon with eggs or eat sausages with eggs?
44. Would you rather eat a baked potato or potato wedges?
45. Would you rather eat scrambled eggs or a fried egg?
46. Would you rather always eat dessert after eating lunch or always eat chips every afternoon?

47. Would you rather drink a glass ice-cold water or a glass of warm water?
48. Would you rather drink a banana smoothie or a blueberry smoothie?
49. Would you rather eat a pretzel or a Pop tart?
50. Would you rather eat cookies or eat crackers?
51. Would you rather eat your favorite food alone or eat an average meal with your best friends?
52. Would you rather only eat food that are colored green or only eat food that are colored red?
53. Would you rather eat steak for a special occasion or eat your favorite pasta dish for a special occasion?
54. Would you rather live beside your favorite restaurant or have your mom cook your favorite dish every week?
55. Would you rather eat brownie batter or cookie dough?
56. Would you rather chew bubble gum or eat a box of jellybeans?
57. Would you rather eat a peach or a nectarine?
58. Would you rather eat onion rings or crab cakes?
59. Would you rather drink a vanilla milkshake or a chocolate milkshake?

60. Would you rather eat a hotdog sandwich every day for the rest of your life or a hamburger every day for the rest of your life?
61. Would you rather eat food with too much garlic or eat food with too much onion?
62. Would you rather drink hot sauce or eat a jalapeno?
63. Would you drink eggnog or drink cider?
64. Would you rather eat a cupcake or a slice of apple pie?
65. Would you ice cream with turkey bits in it or eat a turkey sandwich with ice cream in it?
66. Would you rather never eat meat again or never eat anything with sugar again?
67. Would you rather eat a plate of vegetables or a bowl of fruit?
68. Would you rather eat bacon or eat sausages?
69. Would you rather eat your Mom's favorite food all the time or your Dad's favorite food all the time?
70. Would you rather eat yogurt or drink a glass of milk?
71. Would you rather drink milk with cookies or eat cookie dough ice cream?
72. Would you rather eat frozen yogurt or drink a milk shake?

73. Would you rather eat your favorite leftovers or newly cooked meat loaf?
74. Would you rather eat grapes or an orange?
75. Would you rather be really good at baking cookies or really good at cooking spaghetti?

RANDOM QUESTIONS

1. Would you rather be Thanos or Thor?
2. Would you rather have to hop everywhere or have to run everywhere?
3. Would you rather pet a snake or touch a jellyfish?
4. Would you rather be an expert ice skater or an expert roller skater?
5. Would you rather be a famous dancer or a famous singer?
6. Would you rather watch a funny movie or watch a scary movie?
7. Would you rather be a chef or a server?
8. Would you rather take a long walk or a long bike ride?
9. Would you rather be Superman or Iron Man?
10. Would you rather live in the Sahara desert or in Antartica?

11. Would you rather only ride an elevator or only ride an escalator?
12. Would you rather be a policeman or a soldier?
13. Would you rather play ice hockey or lacrosse?
14. Would you rather be a famous author or a famous musician?
15. Would you rather be a politician or a celebrity?
16. Would you rather live in a hut or in an igloo?
17. Would you rather be a figure skater or an ice hockey player?
18. Would you rather be a solo singer or a member of a band?
19. Would you rather play baseball or basketball?
20. Would you rather live in the mountains or live on the beach?
21. Would you rather play outside in the park or play inside your room?
22. Would you rather go camping or fishing?
23. Would you rather go swimming in a pool or swimming at the beach?
24. Would you rather be a great white shark or a blue whale?
25. Would you rather walk barefoot in a public restroom or walk barefoot on top of poison ivy?

26. Would you rather go to a theme park or a water park?
27. Would you rather go to outer space or explore the ocean?
28. Would you rather be super fast or super strong?
29. Would you rather build a sandcastle or a snow fort?
30. Would you rather it be winter all the time or summer all the time?
31. Would you rather pet a giraffe or pet a rhinoceros?
32. Would you rather go to a birthday party or plan a birthday party?
33. Would you rather celebrate Thanksgiving or celebrate Christmas?
34. Would you rather cook dinner or wash the dishes?
35. Would you rather go down the slide or ride the swing?
36. Would you rather find a turtle in your swimming pool or a frog in your swimming pool?
37. Would you rather live in a treehouse or on a houseboat?
38. Would you rather have a friend forget your birthday or forget your friend's birthday?
39. Would you rather have a headache or a stomachache?

40. Would you rather be a mailman or a meter maid?
41. Would you rather weed the garden or mow the lawn?
42. Would you rather shovel snow or rake leaves?
43. Would you rather get lots of hugs or lots of kisses?
44. Would you rather go to a clothing store or a toy store?
45. Would you rather be in a food fight or watch a food fight?
46. Would you rather take a shower with extra hot water all the time or extra cold water all the time?
47. Would you rather have your own TV in your room or your own Ipad?
48. Would you rather get into a fight with geese or get chased by geese?
49. Would you rather be pranked with a fake spider or pranked with a fake rat?
50. Would you rather turn yourself into a butterfly or turn yourself into a honeybee?
51. Would you rather sleep beside a crocodile or sleep beside a grizzly bear?
52. Would you rather live in a world full of zombies or full of vampires?

53. Would you rather only own one pair of socks or only one pair of pants?
54. Would you rather forget to take your toothbrush for a sleepover or forget to take your towel?
55. Would you rather sleep on a bed of pebbles or a bed of branches?
56. Would you rather go to work with your Mom or go to work with your Dad?
57. Would you rather fall asleep in class or fall asleep in the school bus?
58. Would you rather use soap as shampoo or shampoo as soap?
59. Would you rather lose all your teeth or only have two front teeth?
60. Would you rather have five stitches to fix a cut or have one tooth pulled?
61. Would you rather have no hair at all or hair all over your body?
62. Would you rather never have to toothbrush again or never have to take a bath again?
63. Would you rather ride a bicycle or a skateboard?
64. Would you rather find a pot of gold at the end of a rainbow or a pot of money at the end of a rainbow?
65. Would you rather meet an elf or a fairy?

66. Would you rather play dodgeball or kickball?
67. Would you rather go bungee jumping or sky diving?
68. Would you rather go to Disneyland or to Lego Land?
69. Would you rather sail a boat or ride a hang glider?
70. Would you rather be a captain of a ship or a pilot?
71. Would you rather only be able to walk on all fours or walk sideways like a crab?
72. Would you rather be able to see things that are very far away or magnify everything that you see?
73. Would you rather be a well-loved mascot for a winning team or the coach of a losing team?
74. Would you rather be a fast swimmer or a fast runner?
75. Would you rather win an Olympic medal or an Academy Award?
76. Would you rather be able to run as fast as a cheetah or swim as fast as a shark?
77. Would you rather be really good at Math or really good at sports?
78. Would you rather go on a 6-month cruise or never go on a cruise in your life?
79. Would you rather have your room re-decorated any way you want or buy ten new toys?

80. Would you rather be incredibly lucky or incredibly smart?
81. Would you rather go to Mars or go to the moon?
82. Would you rather have no homework or paid $10 for every hour of homework you do?
83. Would you rather eat one cooked worm or have ten worms crawl on you?
84. Would you rather be a babysitter or a dogsitter?
85. Would you rather play the violin or play the guitar?
86. Would you rather have a best friend who was super smart or a best friend who was super funny?
87. Would you rather own a private island or a luxury yacht?
88. Would you rather move to a different city or move to a different country?
89. Would you rather never have to sleep or never have to eat?
90. Would you rather visit Japan or visit South Korea?
91. Would you rather stay in a cabin or stay in a hotel?
92. Would you rather sneeze uncontrollably for 15 minutes once every day or sneeze once every 3 minutes of the day while you are awake?
93. Would you rather ride a roller coaster or go down a giant water slide?

94. Would you rather go on a one week vacation to a new country every summer vacation or get an extra three weeks of summer break?
95. Would you rather be able to type faster than anyone or read faster than anyone?
96. Would you rather have a giant trampoline or a giant aquarium?
97. Would you rather have no homework or no tests?
98. Would you rather discover a new star or a new planet?
99. Would you rather be an inventor or be the boss of a large company?
100. Would you rather go camping or stay in a hotel room?
101. Would you rather be an eagle or a dolphin?
102. Would you rather build a snowman or a sandcastle?
103. Would you rather live on Mars or live on Jupiter?
104. Would you rather see the future or change the past?
105. Would you rather eat a beetle or get stung by a bee?

106. Would you rather meet a superhero or meet a cartoon character?

107. Would you rather play soccer or baseball?

108. Would you rather discover hidden treasure or discover a living dinosaur?

109. Would you rather have a flying car or a flying chair?

110. Would you rather own your own personal submarine or your own personal airplane?

111. Would you rather have your own robot or your own jetpack?

112. Would you rather own a pet penguin or own a pet ostrich?

113. Would you rather celebrate Christmas every week or celebrate your birthday every month?

114. Would you rather play the trumpet or play the flute?

115. Would you rather read a good book or attend a birthday party?

116. Would you rather live next to your parents in your own house or live with your parents in a mansion for the rest of your life?

117. Would you rather have a pet monkey or be a pet lion?

118.   Would you rather be Mulan or be Jasmine?

119.   Would you rather bungee jump or sky dive?

120.   Would you rather ride a roller coaster or ride a Ferris Wheel?

121.   Would you rather be an animal trainer or a preschool teacher?

122.   Would you rather be an actor in movies or a director of movies?

123.   Would you rather have a sister or have a brother?

124.   Would you rather be famous photographer or be a famous painter?

125.   Would you rather own a big house in a small town or a small house in a big city?

126.   Would you rather travel by plane or travel by hot air balloon?

127.   Would you rather know and understand sign language or have the ability to read lips?

128.   Would you rather own your trampoline or your own bouncy house?

129.   Would you rather look like a fish or smell like a fish?

130.   Would you rather be the oldest child in your family or be the youngest child in your family?

131. Would you rather watch the sunrise or watch the sunset?

132. Would you rather watch Aladdin or Beauty and the Beast?

133. Would you rather watch only your favorite cartoons for the rest of your life or only five other cartoons for the rest of your life?

134. Would you rather have a cold winter that lasts for two weeks or a mild winter that lasts for two months?

135. Would you rather live on a farm or live on mansion?

136. Would you rather be a plumber or a roofer?

137. Would you rather be a race car driver or a jet ski racer?

138. Would you rather read ten books or color ten pictures?

139. Would you rather have detention every day for two months or go to summer school?

140. Would you rather be a pediatrician or a veterinarian?

141. Would you rather swim in a pool of marshmallows or a swim in a pool of M&Ms?

142. Would you rather step on a crab or touch a jellyfish?

143. Would you rather play with sand or play with clay?

144. Would you rather own a supermarket or own a school?

145. Would you rather color a picture with paint or color a picture with crayons?

146. Would you rather go on an African safari or go backpacking on Mount Everest?

147. Would you rather ride in a convertible or the back of a motorcycle?

148. Would you rather clear the table or clean your room?

149. Would you rather be named after your dad's parents or your mom's parents?

150. Would you rather work in an airport or work in a bank?

151. Would you rather watch a two-hour movie or two hours of shows?

152. Would you rather be a deep sea diver or be an astronaut?

153. Would you rather be an expert at coding or learn to speak two new languages?

154. Would you rather live in a house with no windows or live in a house with no doors?
155. Would you rather go on a long airplane ride or a long train ride?
156. Would you rather go surfing or skiing?
157. Would you rather be a flight attendant or work in a cruise ship?
158. Would you rather have a playdate with your classmates or have a playdate with your cousins?
159. Would you rather travel one hour to go to school every day or be homeschooled?
160. Would you be a dentist or a doctor?
161. Would you rather travel around the world alone or stay home with your family?
162. Would you rather create a new holiday or a new language?
163. Would you rather be a tutor or be a guidance counselor?
164. Would you rather wake up your Mom early in the morning or wake up your Dad early in the morning?
165. Would you rather have ten mosquito bites or one bee sting?

166. Would you rather grow vegetables in your garden or have lots of flowers in your garden?

167. Would you rather dance or draw?

168. Would you rather go to the zoo or go to a children's museum?

169. Would you rather have a pet panda or a pet Polar bear?

170. Would you rather sleep on a big but hard bed or small but soft bed?

CONCLUSION

Yay! You've made it to the end of the book. We hope you had lots of fun asking and answering the hundreds of *Would You Rather* questions we prepared for you. Some of the questions have been staples of Would You Rather games around the world, and some are original questions we've come up with ourselves. We included both types to make sure you had a great time playing. Don't forget, you can use this book over and over again, especially if you have a new group of friends or other family members to play with

Again, we'd like to thank you for buying and supporting our book *The Would You Rather Game Book for Kids*. Did you enjoy our questions? We hope you did! Please leave us a review and let us know your thoughts and how much fun you had. We'd really appreciate it! Reviews are very important to us and they'll help us create more books like this in the future.

Thank you!

Made in the USA
Middletown, DE
12 November 2020

23802549R00035